Poems
I Wrote
While Taking
A Shit

TAMARA YAJIA

For Nat.

Untitled Fart

A long fart
Comes to an end
Silence fills the bathroom
Another fart arrives
Short and choppy
Silence again

My Body Is A Meatloaf

My body is a meatloaf.
A rectangular
chunk
Of solidified lard.
My body is a meatloaf.
It resembles
The armoire from
Beauty and The Beast.
A sturdy
Block
Of mass.

My body is a meatloaf.
Take a bite
My darling
But beware
I over did it with the garlic.
So cover your mouth
When you burp me out.

A Night Of Passion

I wake up
Covered in sweat
In my adobe casita.

The oppressive heat
Of the jungle
Surrounds my nude
And naked body.

The sound of a thousand cicadas
Doing their magical dance
As they mate
Within their species.

But wait.
I hear another sound
Coming from outside.
Footsteps.
Rustling of leaves.
I am all alone
And fearful
But a little bit horny
Because I am ovulating.

I feel feral.
Dressed in nothing
But my pubic bush.

He is here for me.
A beast.
The Chupacabra.
His penis a long,
Erect,
Green,
Rod
Ready
To fornicate me.

Sail Away

A sublime
Ocean Liner
Sails
Across the open,
Glistening waters.
The Skies
Clear.
The wind
Brisk and crisp.
My mother
My father
My sister
And I
Share a cabin
The size of a closet
With four bunkbeds.

It smells like a foot.

Star Wars

George Lucas
Head so big
Like a giant's nipple

What My Hand
Feels Like
After I Eat
Too Much Salt.

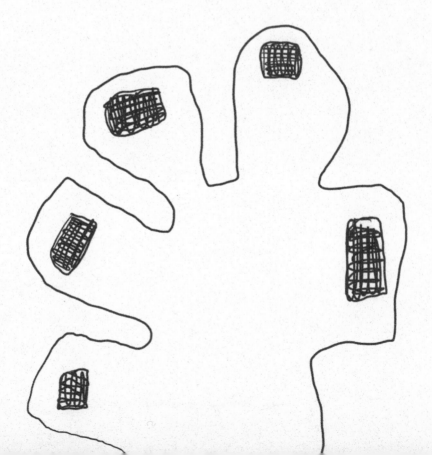

Antonio Banderas

Mi amor!
I have loved you
Ever since I was a girl,
When Madonna put you in
Her "Take a Bow"
Music video.
She saw a light in you,
And so do I.

Please,
Be with me
My strong and lean
Spanish papazuelo.

Let us defeat the bulls together.
You can protect me with your red
Cape.

Antonio,
Mi amor!
I bet you have a beautiful pelvis.
You trim your pubes
Regularly.
Your abs,
Hard like
The bottoms of tap shoes.

I want you to be the
Don Quixote
To my Sancho Panza.
We will
Gallop into the sunset
As one.
Antonio,
Mi amorcito.
Give me un besito
In my pussy.

I Can Never Win

On Monday morning mother texted me:
"Wish Betina Rabinovich a happy birthday."

On Tuesday morning mother texted me:
"Wish your cousin Ezequiel Aizenberg a happy birthday."

On Wednesday morning mother texted me:
"Wish Martha Talpini-Gomez a happy birthday"

On Thursday morning mother texted me:
"Wish your father in law a happy birthday."

On Friday morning,
I wake up at 6 AM
Determined to beat my mother at this game.

I check Facebook
To gather intel
Regarding whose birthday it is.

I learn that it's Alberto Friedman's birthday.
My great uncle,
Who once was caught fingering his maid.
Regardless,
I visit Alberto's Facebook page.
"Happy Birthday!"
I write.

I then text my mother:
"Today is Uncle Alberto's birthday."
I have defeated her,
For once.

I buzz with pride.

My mother texts back:
"Uncle Alberto died three years ago."

Untitled Cheese

How disgusting is it
When you touch
An object
That smells
Like cheese
But
Isn't cheese

Not Horny Right Now

I'm not connecting with my genitals
Right now
Or anyone else's
To be honest.
I have very little motivation
To touch a penis
And absolutely
No motivation
To touch balls.

The Climbing Of
Mount Bunion

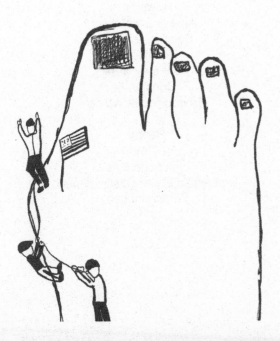

A Detailed Description of The Seven Dwarf's Nipples

Doc.
Burgundy areolas
Big like coasters.

Dopey.
Two fat meatballs.
An abundance of
Texture.
Unappealing to look at.

Bashful.
Pert.
Rarely erect.
Surrounded by dainty
Peach fuzz.

Sneezy.
No one knows,
As he has never been seen
Without a top.
There is,
However,
Always a wetness
Seeping through
His blouse.
As if they were
Constantly
Producing discharge.

Happy.
Tiny
Like papercuts.
That emit a slight whistling sound
When pinched.

Sleepy
High levels of estrogen.
Plump.
An Intoxicating smell of
Talcum powder.

Grumpy.
Pierced,
Always erect,
And noticeably
Chewed on.

If you're shitting while reading this, please use this page to draw a picture of what your turd looks like. If you're not shitting, please use this page to draw a picture of the Property Brothers.

Jacuzzi

Jacuzzi.
Large toilet
For the body
Some people faint inside.
Too much cum

A Chapter Dedicated to My Husband

Shrek

I just walked into My living room
And found
My husband
Sitting in
Complete darkness
Holding
An onion.

Hey my love

If my husband screams
"Hey my love"
From the bathroom
It means he needs
Me to grab him
Toilet paper
To wipe the shit
From his ass.

Not Interested

My husband
Bought
Two Dollars Worth of
Bitcoin
And now
He speaks
An entire new language
That Sounds Like
Klingon.
Not Interested.

No control over his sphincter

This Man's
Farts
Fall out of his ass
Like coins
Fall out of
A pocket
With a hole in it.

I Love You, My Husband

We watch Pixar shorts
Together
And Cry

I Started Drawing
Intestines And It Took Me
Somewhere Else.

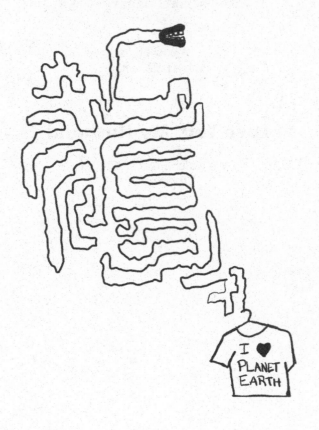

Cystic Acne

Cystic acne
During my teenage years.
Hot and hard like cement.
A curse from Satan.
Why do this to me
At my most vulnerable
Hormonal
And
Insecure
Time.

I felt hideous.
My chin, cheeks, and sometimes neck
Felt like they had
Wrecking balls
Under the skin.
Volcanos,
Dying to erupt
And release
Geysers of pus,
Oh what pressure there was behind them!
BURNING PAIN.

I Felt like shit.
I would try to pop them.
And sometimes they'd explode onto my mirror.
A Jackson Pollock painting.
But most of the time,
they refused to exit my body,
Clinging to the flesh,
Not ready to face the world
Without my body
As their vehicle.

Cystic Acne
During my teenage years.
Hot and hard like cement.

Jason Momoa

Jason Momoa
How are you baby?
I'm well.
How are your pecks?
Good?
That's great.
I hope you are feeling strong.
Jason Momoa
Jason Momomoa.

Died Too Soon

Esophagus.
Long tube.
I am not nice to it.

Esophagus.
Slippery pipe.
It burns day and night.

Esophagus.
Wet cylinder.
A piece of corn sticks to it
And leads to my death.

That Little Cartoon Meme of The Dog

That little
Cartoon meme
Of the dog
Sitting in a room
That's on fire
Saying
"This is fine"
Depresses me.
I don't think it's funny.
I don't think it's amusing.
I hate it.
I'm sick of seeing it.
Don't send it to me.

Pubes In The Wind

Fútbol

Lionel Messi
Master of Fútbol
Quick little feet
And fast legs
He was once told he was
Too short
To play soccer.
Look at him now.
A master
Of goals.
This poem sucks.
I am insecure.
I can't play soccer.
One time I scored against my own team.
I could see my father sitting in the sidelines.
Covering his face with his hands.
Pure embarrassment.
I was 12.
I wasn't paying attention.
It was the first and last goal
I ever scored.

A Chapter Dedicated to Different Types of Tits

Great Tits

My house is a disaster
My life is a disaster
My finances are a disaster
My face is a disaster
But my tits look great

Informed Tit

I'm watching
Prime Time with Chris Cuomo
With one of my tits out.
Breaking News!
He says.
My nipples perk up.
They are
Curious about
The state of the World.

Hard Tits

About to get my period
My tits hurt
Like hell
Two Cantaloupes
Heavy like bowling balls
I'm a fertile goddess.
Honk, Honk.

Soft Tits

My breasts are very soft
And silky
Like two
Sleeping doves
Cooo ruuuuu
Cooo ruuuuu

Saggy Tits

Grandmother.
Mother of my mother.
Life giver.
Tits so saggy.
She can wrap them around
Her neck
Like a scarf.

Feelings

I don't wanna go to therapy tonight
I don't wanna go to therapy tonight
I really don't wanna go to therapy tonight
But I probably should go to therapy tonight.

Grandpa's Balls

The first testicles I ever saw
Were my grandpa's.
Boingy, boingy.

I was around 10 years old
When he took my sister and I
To Mervyn's.
Boingy, boingy.

The two of us ended up in the dressing room with him
while he tried on shorts.
That's when I noticed his saggy balls,
Hanging from below his boxer shorts.
They hung to his knees
And looked like nun-chucks.
Boingy, boingy.

My mom hates it when I tell people this story.
She says it makes him look pervy.
She told me I'm making the memory up,
Which is not true,
Because my sister remembers it
As well.
Boingy, boingy.

911

When I feel manic
I have this urge
To pull my pants down
At work
And take a shit
On the floor
In front of my coworkers.

I Just Got This Text From An Unknown

Riverdance

I love Riverdance
Takatakataka

All those tiny feet
Moving in various directions
Takatakataka

So much happening on the stage
My brain can't keep up
Takatakataka

Hands on their hips
The foot goes up
The foot goes criss cross
It's not quite tap dancing
Takatakataka

My laziness prevents me
From doing this sort of dance
But at least I'm not too lazy
To clap along with my hands
When the fiddle kicks in
Takatakataka

This Poem Depresses Me

There once was an old woman
That used to come into my work
Who had a skinny
Long
Beard
And no teeth
Except for one
Rotting tooth that stuck out
Of the front of her mouth

The tooth always reminded me
Of Cinderella's mouse friend
Gus
For some reason

I always think about that woman's tooth
Because the day will come
When I too
Lose all my teeth.
I don't think I'll make it to old age
With all of them.
My grandparents all had dentures.
We do not have good dental genes
I already have receding gums
Our teeth just fall right out.

Once
My grandmother had her hip replaced.
She was being wheeled
Out of the operating room
After her surgery
And was still high from the
Anesthetic.

She looked like a monster
Without her teeth in.
Her entire face had sunken in.
She was a Muppet.

We all waved
As they rolled her past us
And she looked at us and said
Some words that none of us understood.

My aunt had dentures too
She would make us bring her
Denture adhesive paste
Whenever we visited her in Argentina.
"The national brands don't hold as well"
She would tell us.
So we would travel from the United States
With 3 dozen packs
Of Fixodent
In our suitcases.

When she died.
I had to recognize her body
At the morgue.
She was barely recognizable
Without her dentures.

Commute

Headed home from work.
No Traffic.
A feeling of freedom.
Wind hits my face.

A putrid smell of cheese rot.

Ode To MSNBC

MSNBC
A channel of liberal news
That I enjoy.
Thank you, Thank you.

Alone after work
And in the morning
While I drink my coffee
With almond milk
And eat a hard-boiled egg.
What a delight.
Thank you, Thank you.

Their afternoon lineup
Goes like this:
Hardball with Chris Matthews.
Why is that show named that?
Thank you, Thank you.

All in with Chris Hayes.
There's something attractive about him.
He follows me on Instagram.
Seems like a nice guy.
Thank you, Thank you.

The Rachel Maddow Show
My favorite of the bunch.
Great investigative work.
You go girl.
Thank you, Thank you.

Last word with Lawrence O'Donnell.
Looks kind of like a penis.
Thank you, Thank you.

11th Hour with Brian Williams.
Kind of looks like
Lawrence O'Donnell.
Two penises.
Back to back.
Thank you,
Thank you.

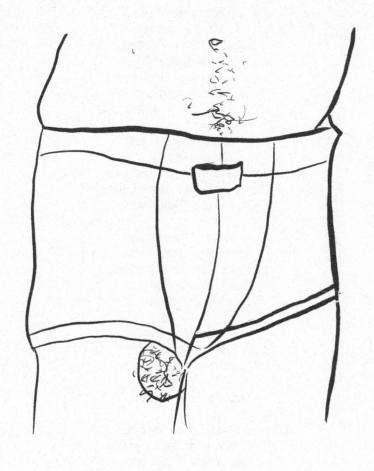

My Nut Slipped Out

Closeness

Yesterday
I asked
My psychologist
To smell
My Armpit

Dream On

A tooth falls out of
Steven Tyler's mouth
While singing
"Dream On"
And lands on the whiskey and coke
Of a man
In the front row
Who promised himself
He wouldn't drink tonight.

Medicine Cabinet

There's nothing more beautiful
and awe inspiring
than a fully stocked medicine cabinet.
I'd rather stand in front of a medicine cabinet
Than in front of the
Grand Canyon.
If you've invited me to your home,
I've probably looked through your medicine cabinet.
Even if I don't steal something
I love to poke around and look at what my friends are taking.
For the most part
it's allergy medications.
If you're smart,
and an addict like me,
you know to keep the good,
fun pills in a second location
that no one knows about.

I Look like Exactly Like
Charlize Theron*

* When she played Aileen Wournos in Monster.

My Landlord Bob's
Elegant Legs

Chewed Chunk Of Food

A piece of food
Flew from someone's mouth,
Landed
Directly on my forearm
And neither of us
Acknowledged it.

A Poem Inspired by The Hit TV Show "Outlander"

In the Scottish forest
I sit by a fire
Warming my hands.
I am a maiden
Cold and alone.
A strong Scottish lad approaches
Muscles aplenty,
Hair red like apples.
"Young lass, I will keep ye warm"
He says,
As he lifts his kilt
And places his hot nutsack
On my shivering face.

Bon Appetite

Invited friends over for dinner.
Can't cook for shit.
Gonna serve
Them oranges
And tell
Them it's
A delicacy.

And Now, A Variety Pack Sampler Of Poems About Cured Meats

Grandfather's Illness

The gout is here
Tralalá Tralalá
Grandpa refused to cut blood sausages
From his diet
Now his toe throbs in agony

Untitled 1

Jamón Serrano
Jamón Serrano
Thin flaps of slippery goodness.
One time my sister ate too many slices
And vomited.

Untitled 2

Liverwurst
A lighter color sausage.
Reminds me
Of a Beluga whale.

Safety First

A sausage
So long
You can use it
As a seatbelt.

That's A No from Me

What's the deal with Pancetta?
Small cubes of pork bits.
I don't like them
That much.

Loss and Grief

Two dry salamis
Inside my purse
Ready to be enjoyed.
I long to get home
And share them with my husband.
But first,
I stop at a bar
For a friend's birthday party.
The doorman asks to look inside my bag.
He sees the salamis,
Then points to a sign on the door
"No outside food allowed."
He reaches into my bag
And confiscates my delicious meats.
I am filled with blind rage.

Two Vaginas

KD Lang
And I
On a merry go round
Riding on
The back of
A swan.
Our vaginas,
Wet.

Portrait Of Nude Woman

Handing You A Hot Cheeto

Choads

My organic friend
Grew some organic squashes
In her organic gardens
That look like
Choads.

Tonsil Stones

A couple times per year
A little white stone comes out
Of my throat.
It just
Pops right out.
So I cough it out of my mouth,
And crush it with my fingers.
It smells like death.

Untitled Fart (continued)

A long fart
Comes to an end.

Silence fills the bathroom.

Another fart arrives.
Short and choppy.

Silence again.

I am determined to shit.

It's been two days
Since my last bowel movement.

Pain.

I remove all my clothes,
Take a deep breath,
And squeeze
With all my strength
Letting out a biblical scream.

I am Hercules
I am Nefertiti
I am The Rock Dwayne Johnson
I am Mother Earth
I AM TAMARA YAJIA
I have given birth
To a stillborn,
Glistening
Turd.

Mood Swings

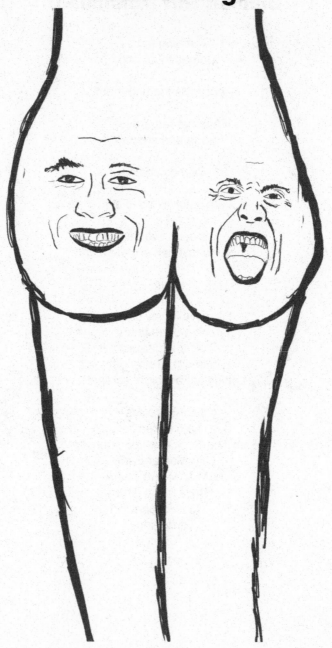

I want to thank the amazing Mark Duplass for making this book happen. Thank you Mom and Dad. Thank you Pat for marrying me. Lastly, thank you to Julie Peterson for helping me put this book together, I couldn't have done it without you.

And Thank YOU, Antonio Banderas.

Design By Julie Peterson
Artwork By Tamara Yajia